LONELY PLANET'S
WILD WORLD

Melbourne | London | Oakland

IT'S A
WILD
WORLD

What do you feel when you stand somewhere breathtakingly wild?
Or as a tropical thunderstorm crashes cataclysmically overheard
or when a heavy wave smashes on a remote shore? For many, it's a
combination of peacefulness and exhilaration. England's Romantic
poets described these natural experiences, those that inspired awe,
reverence and an almost transcendental emotional response, as
'the sublime'. They sought these reveries, often alone, walking in
England's Lake District and beyond, in Europe's alpine regions.

This book is intended to share some of every continents' most
sublime corners, from the Arctic's tundra to the great deserts of
central Asia, from the world's largest cave to its wind-whipped
mountain peaks. We'll meet some of the planet's quirkier residents
and be immersed in its most extraordinary natural phenomena.

Scientific studies repeatedly show that being in nature decreases
stress. We feel mentally invigorated, spiritually connected, and more
optimistic in the wild. Indeed, if we don't get outdoors enough we may
even suffer from 'nature deficit disorder', a term coined by author
Richard Louv. These photographs will take you to wonderful places,
far and wide, and inspire new journeys off the beaten track.

Curating this book, it was clear that humans have left their mark
on almost every inch of the globe, from the rainforests of South
America and Africa to the oceans' reefs. But, despite all the
changes we have wrought upon it, our home still has the power
to evoke awe, respect, passion and protectiveness, to comfort and
thrill us, to change our lives. Billions of years after it was forged,
it's still a wild world.

~ AFRICA ~

Sunset over Sossusvlei. **Namib-Naukluft National Park, Namibia**

Diademed sifaka. **Madagascar**

African Pyramids. **Begrawiya, Sudan** ➤ |

Cattle egret and Cape buffalo. **Duba Plains, Okavango Delta, Botswana** ^ |

Rolling sea of sand. **Rub' al-Khali, Oman** ➤ |

Flamingos take flight. **South Africa**   ^ |

Lioness scatters vultures. **Cottars Conservancy, Kenya** ^

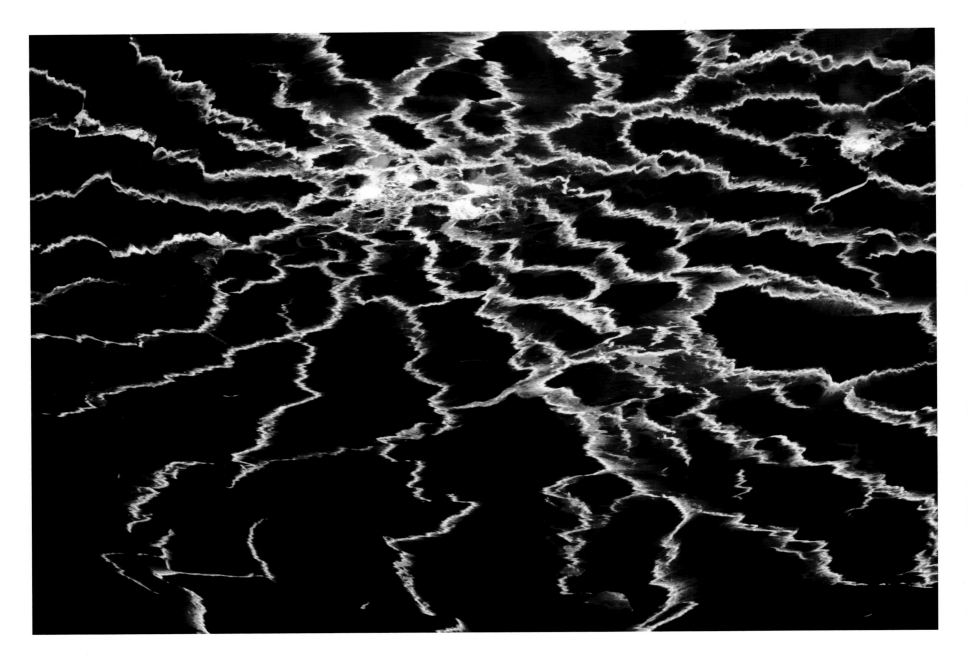

Nyiragongo Volcano. **Democratic Republic of the Congo** ⌃ |

Quiver Tree. **Namibia** ^

Elephants on the move. **Garamba National Park, Democratic Republic of the Congo**

Gathering storm. **Maasai Mara, Kenya**

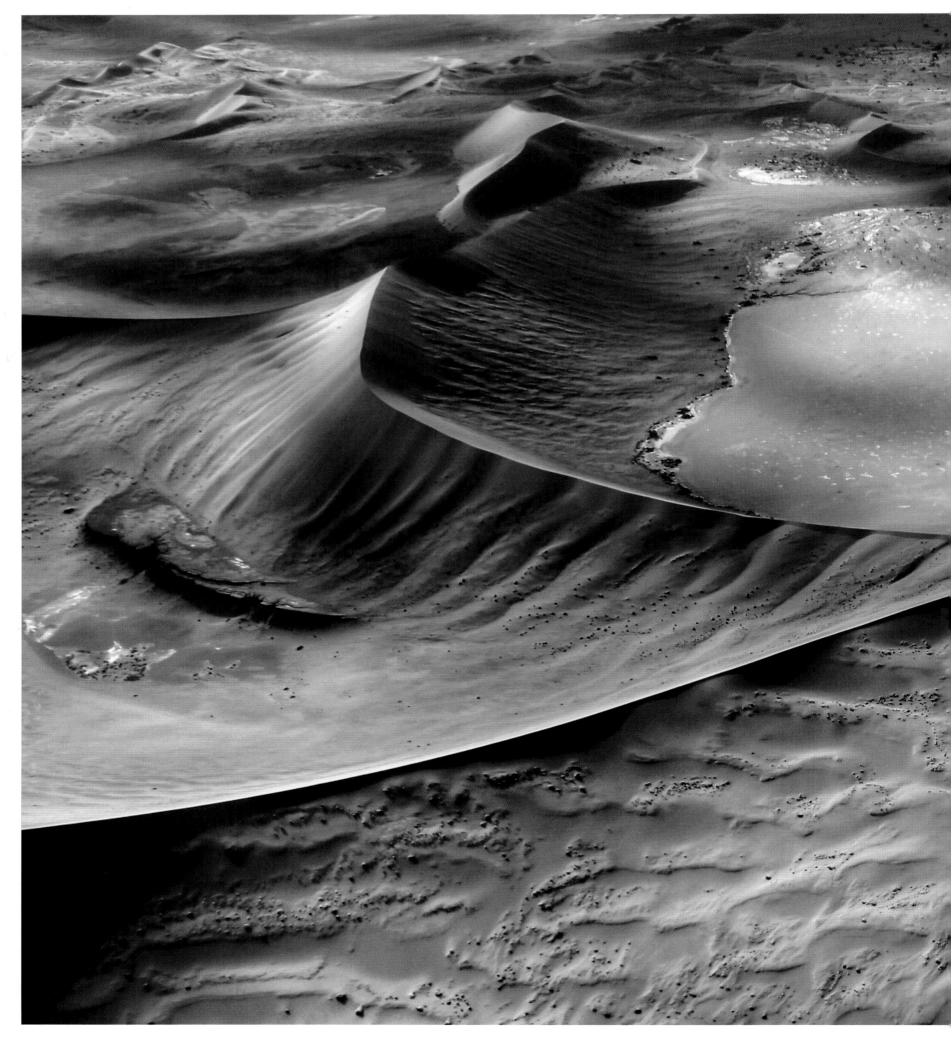

Dune dreamscape. **Namib Desert, Namibia** ∧ |

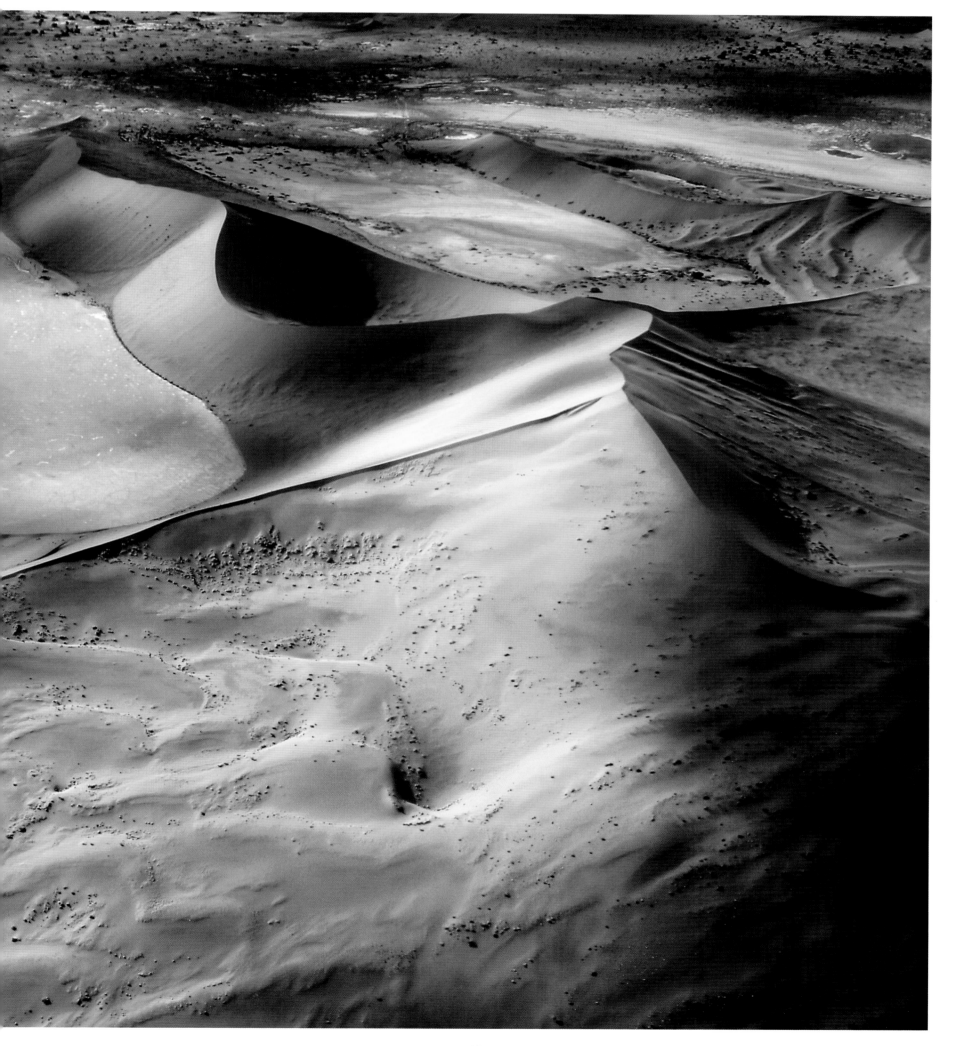

Brandberg Massif. **Damaraland, Namibia** ▲ |

Southern carmine bee-eater. **Zambezi River, Namibia** ⌃ |

Straw-coloured fruit bats roosting. **Kasanka National Park, Zambia** ^ |

Fruit bats in the evening. **Kasanka National Park, Zambia** ∧ |

Hoggar mountains. **Algeria** ⌃ |

Sailfish eyeing sardines. **Port St John, South Africa**

Murchison Falls. **Murchison Falls National Park, Uganda**   ▲

Fighting male gemsboks. **Etosha National Park, Namibia** ⌃ |

Blue gnu. **Kenya** ^ |

Simien Mountains. **Ethiopia** ⌃ |

Gaberoun oasis. **Idehan Ubari, Libya** ^ |

~ EUROPE ~

Matterhorn and Zermatt. **Switzerland** ^ |

Lofoten wall and village. **Nordland, Norway** ›

Eurasian wolf. **Norway**   ^ |

Federa Lake. **The Dolomites, Italy** ^ |

Metéora rock formations. **Central Greece** ⌃ |

The Cliffs of Moher. **County Clare, Ireland** ⌃ |

Galloping reindeer herd. **Swedish Lapland**

Lago di Carezza. **The Dolomites, Italy** ∧

Serra de Tramuntana. **Mallorca, Spain** ›

Icebergs. **Jökulsárlón, Iceland** ⌃ |

Geirangerfjord and Seven Sisters waterfall. **Sunnmøre, Norway** ⌃ |

Landmannalaugar. **Fjallabak Nature Reserve, Iceland** ❯

Simeto River. **Sicily, Italy** ^ |

Central Balkan National Park. **Bulgaria** ^ |

Great white pelicans. **Danube Delta, Romania** ^ |

Karwendel Range. **Bavarian Alps, Germany**

Fajã Grande, Flores Island. **Azores, Portugal** ⌃ |

Autumnal forest. **Velebit, Croatia** ^ |

Holuhraun eruption. **Highlands, Iceland** ^ |

Red kite in flight. **Chiltern Hills, England** ▲ |

Icelandic horse. **Iceland** ^ |

Col de Bavella. **Corsica, France** ^ |

Atlantic coast, Cornwall. **England, UK** ^ |

Life at Land's End. **Cornwall, England** ▲ |

Snowdonia. **North Wales** ^ |

- ASIA -

Crystal Cave. **Dead Sea, Jordan** ⌃ |

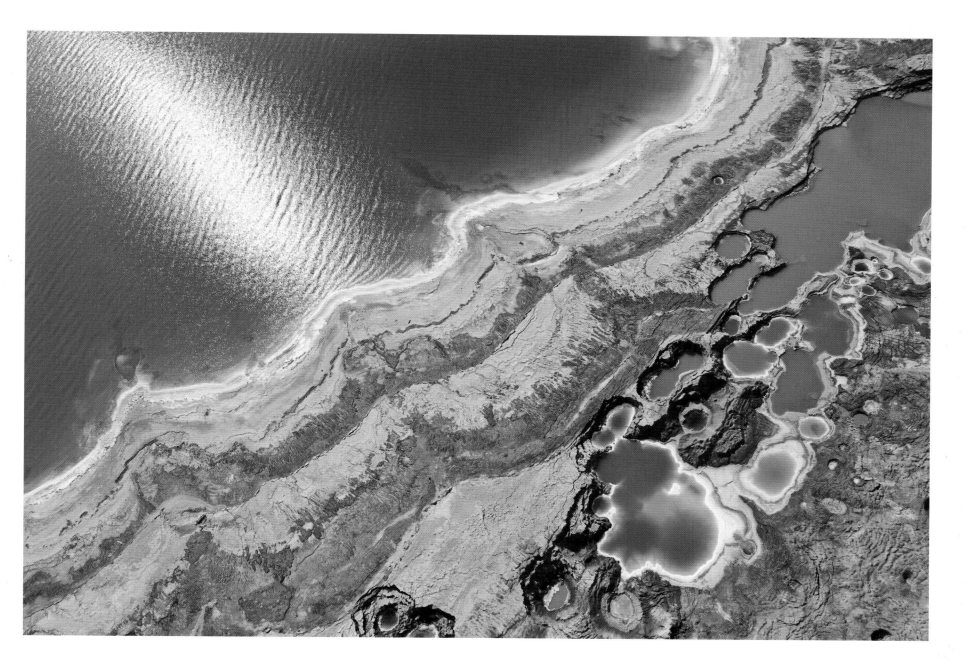

Dead Sea shore. **Ein Gedi, Israel** ^ |

Break dancing. **Nias Island, North Sumatra** ∧ |

Longtailed macaque. **Bali, Indonesia** ^ |

Juvenile gaur. **Kanha National Park, Madhya Pradesh, India**

Huangshan Mountains. **Anhui, China** ᴧ |

Forest of the fireflies. **Okayama, Japan**

Camels up close. **Gansu Province, China** ^ |

Ships of the desert. **Badain Jaran, Mongolia** ^ |

Valley of the Geysers. **Kamchatka, Russia** ▲ |

Rocks and rollers. **Lampung, Indonesia**   ^ |

Rose Valley. **Cappadocia, Turkey** ⌃ |

Potanina Glacier. **Altai Tavan Bogd National Park, Mongolia** ˄

Kaluts at sunrise. **Iran** ⌃ |

Bubble coral shrimp. **Bunaken National Marine Park, Indonesia** ⌃ | Cathedral of coral. **Bunaken National Marine Park, Indonesia** ›

Korowai tribesman. **Southeastern Papua, Indonesia** ^ |

~ AUSTRALASIA ~

Termite tower. **East Kimberley, Western Australia** ^ |

Heron among boulders. **Otago, South Island, New Zealand** ^ |

White Island. **Bay of Plenty, New Zealand** ∧ |

Whale encounter. **Kaikoura, South Island, New Zealand** ⌃ |

Bouncing kangaroos. **Cape Le Grand, Western Australia** ^

Giant barrel sponge. **Papua New Guinea** ＾ |

Windswept macrocarpas. **The Catlins, South Island, New Zealand**   ᴧ |

Portuguese-man-o-war. **Australia** ^ |

Hill Inlet, Whitsunday Islands National Park. **Queensland, Australia** ^ |

Bungle Bungle Range. **Purnululu National Park, Western Australia** ^ |

Lesser Bird of Paradise. **Papua New Guinea** ^ |

Curio Bay rollers. **South Island, New Zealand** ⌃ |

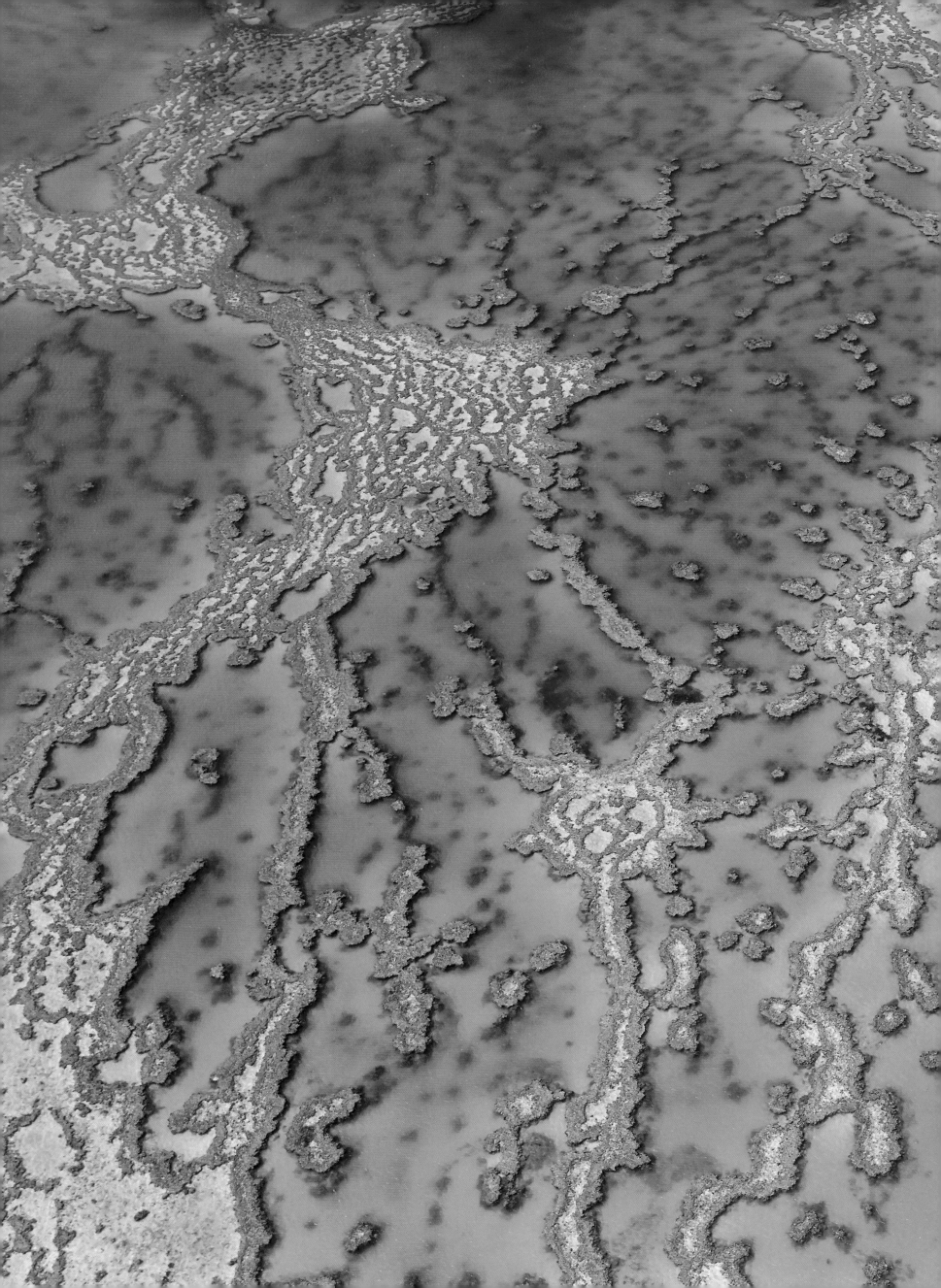

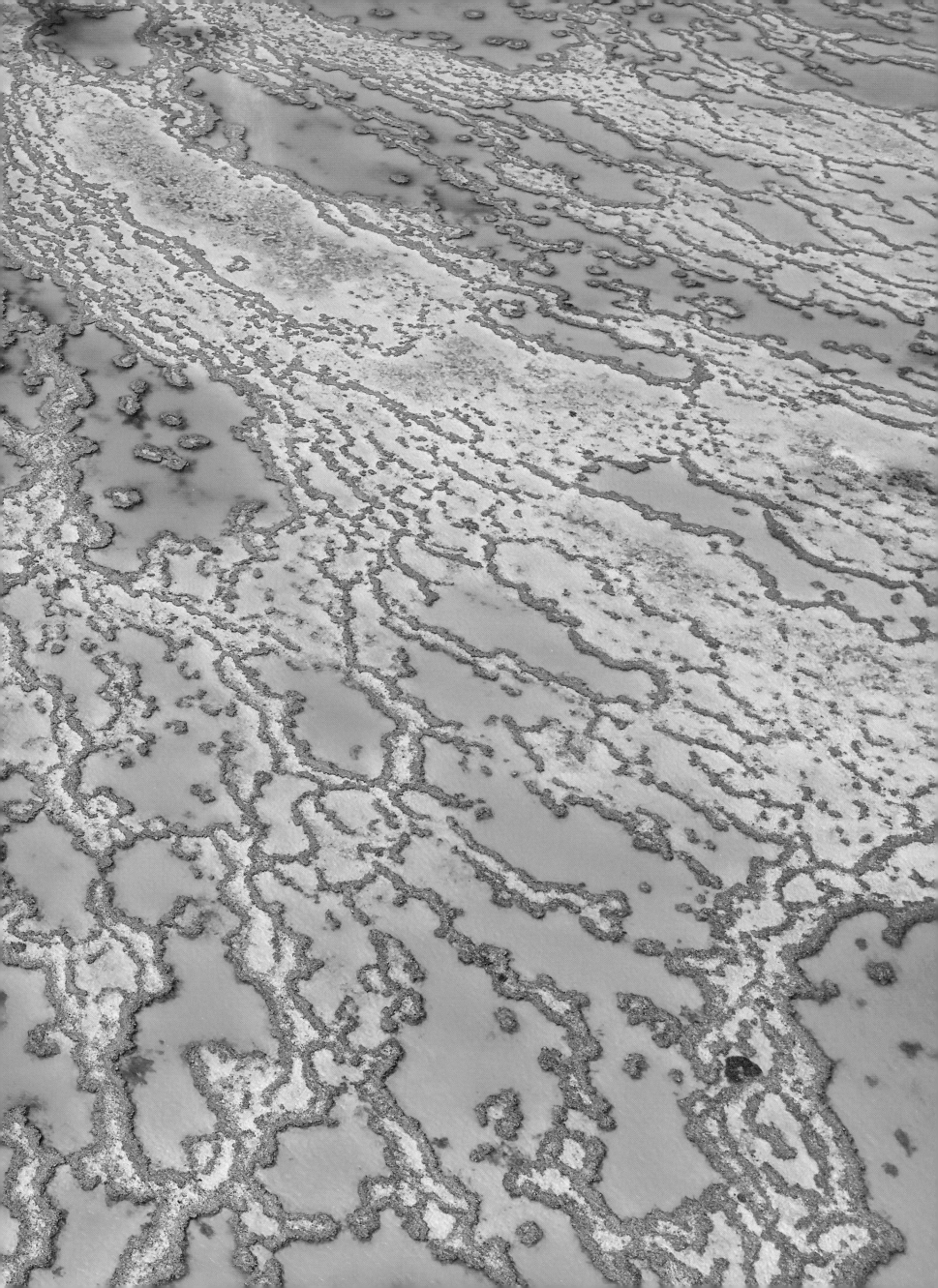

Cassowary. **Australia** ⌃ |

Russle lupines. **Lake Tekapo, South Island, New Zealand** ^ |

Twisted tea tree. **Mornington Wildlife Sanctuary, Australia**   ^ |

The Corner of the World. **Nugget Point, South Island, New Zealand** ⌄

Kahurangi National Park. **South Island, New Zealand** ^ |

Lightning strike. **Queensland, Australia** ^ |

~ ANTARCTICA ~

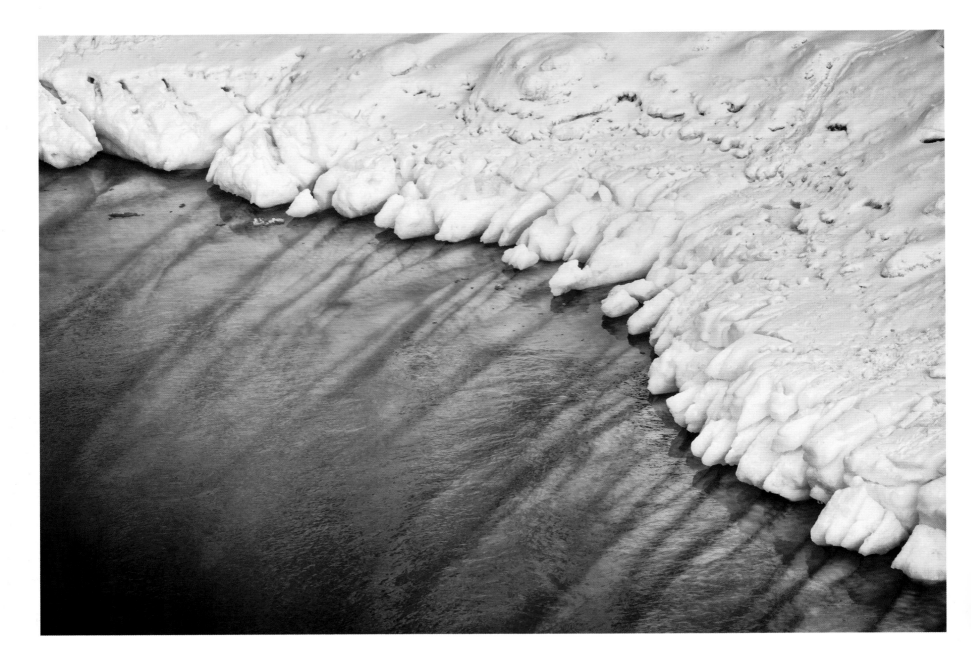

Iceberg. **Antarctic Peninsula** ^ |

Gentoo penguin. **Antarctica** ^ |

An ice flow with seal. **Wilhelmina Bay, Antarctica** ^ |

King penguins. **South Georgia** ⌃

~ SOUTH AMERICA ~

Jaguar. **South America**   ⌃ |

Waterlilies at sunrise. **Pantanal, Brazil** ^

Parque Nacional dos Lençóis Maranhenses. **Maranhão, Brazil** ˄ |

Park Nacional Natural Tayrona. **Colombia** ^ |

Desert camelids. **Atacama Desert, Chile** ⌃ |

Rio de Janeiro. **Brazil**

Poison frog. **Río Marañón, Peru** ∧ |

Iguazu Falls. **Brazil** ▲ |

Shoal of piraputanga. **Mato Grosso do Sul, Brazil** ⌃ |

Eruption of Calbuco. **Los Lagos, Chile** ^ |

Toucan. **Cartagena, Colombia**

Yavarí River. **The Amazon, Peru** ⌃

Moai. **Easter Island, Chile** ^ |

Pailón del Diablo. **Baños de Agua Santa, Ecuador** › |

Paine massif. **Torres del Paine, Chile** ⌃ |

Whitewater kayaker. **Rio Azul, Chile** ∧

Andean condor. **Colca Canyon, Peru** ⌃ |

Galápagos sea lion. **Galápagos Islands, Ecuador** ⌃ |

Hummingbird drawing. **Nazca, Peru** ⌃ |

~ NORTH AMERICA ~

Cactus. **Mexico** ∧ |

Excelsior geyser. **Yellowstone National Park, Wyoming, USA** › |

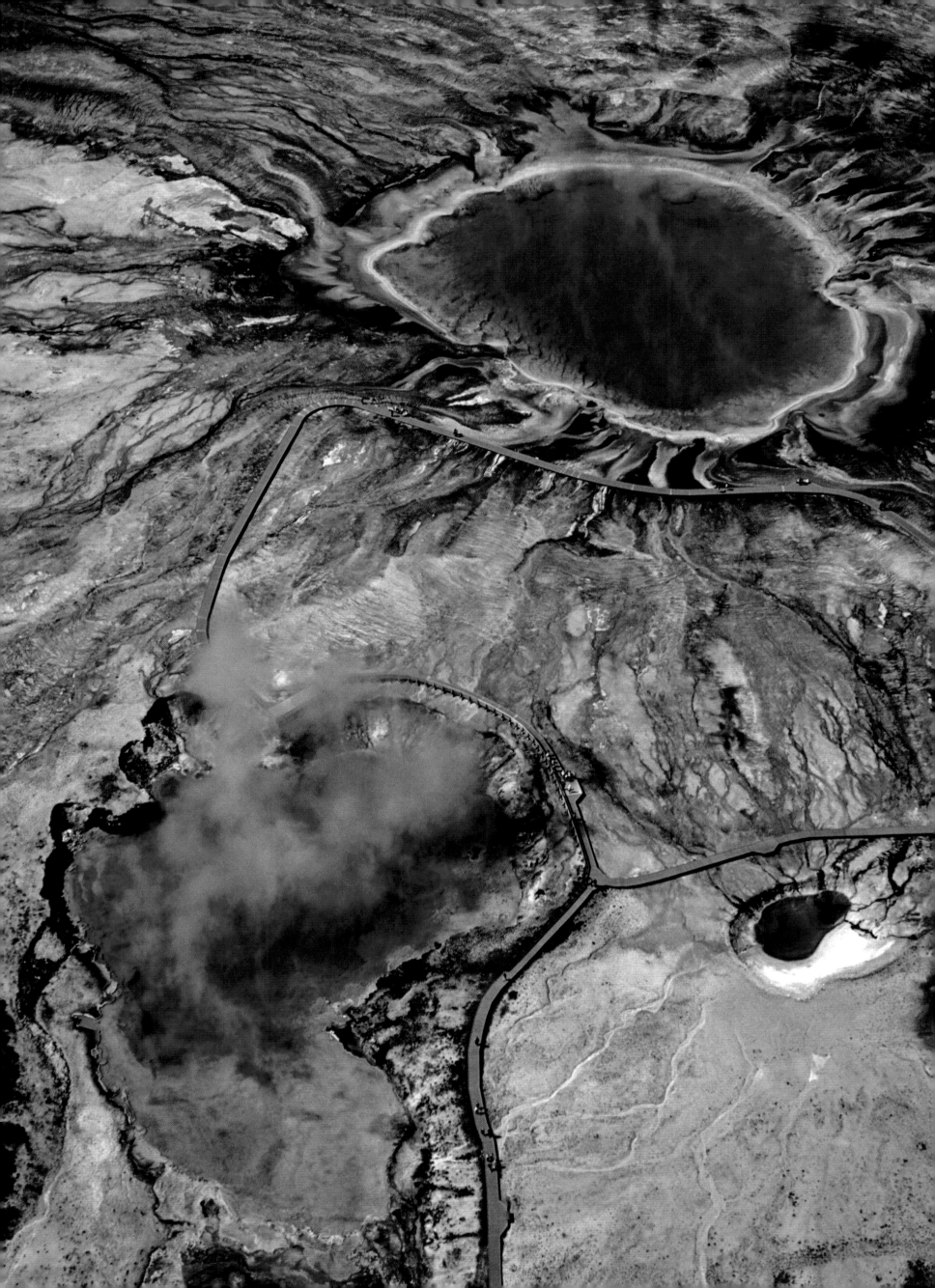

Sol Duc Falls. **Washington, USA** ^

Whaler's Grave. **Marble Island, Hudson Bay, Canada** ▴ |

Grey Whale. **British Columbia, Canada** ⌃ |

Na Pali Coast. **Kaua'i, Hawaii** ∧ |

Glacier patterns. **Wrangell-St Elias National Park, Alaska** ⌃ |

Trafalgar Falls. **Dominica** ^ |

Peggy's Cove. **Nova Scotia, Canada** ᐱ |

Cape Race. **Newfoundland, Canada** ᐳ |

Polar bear. **Hudson Bay, Canada** ^ |

The Narrows. **Zion National Park, Utah, USA** ^ |

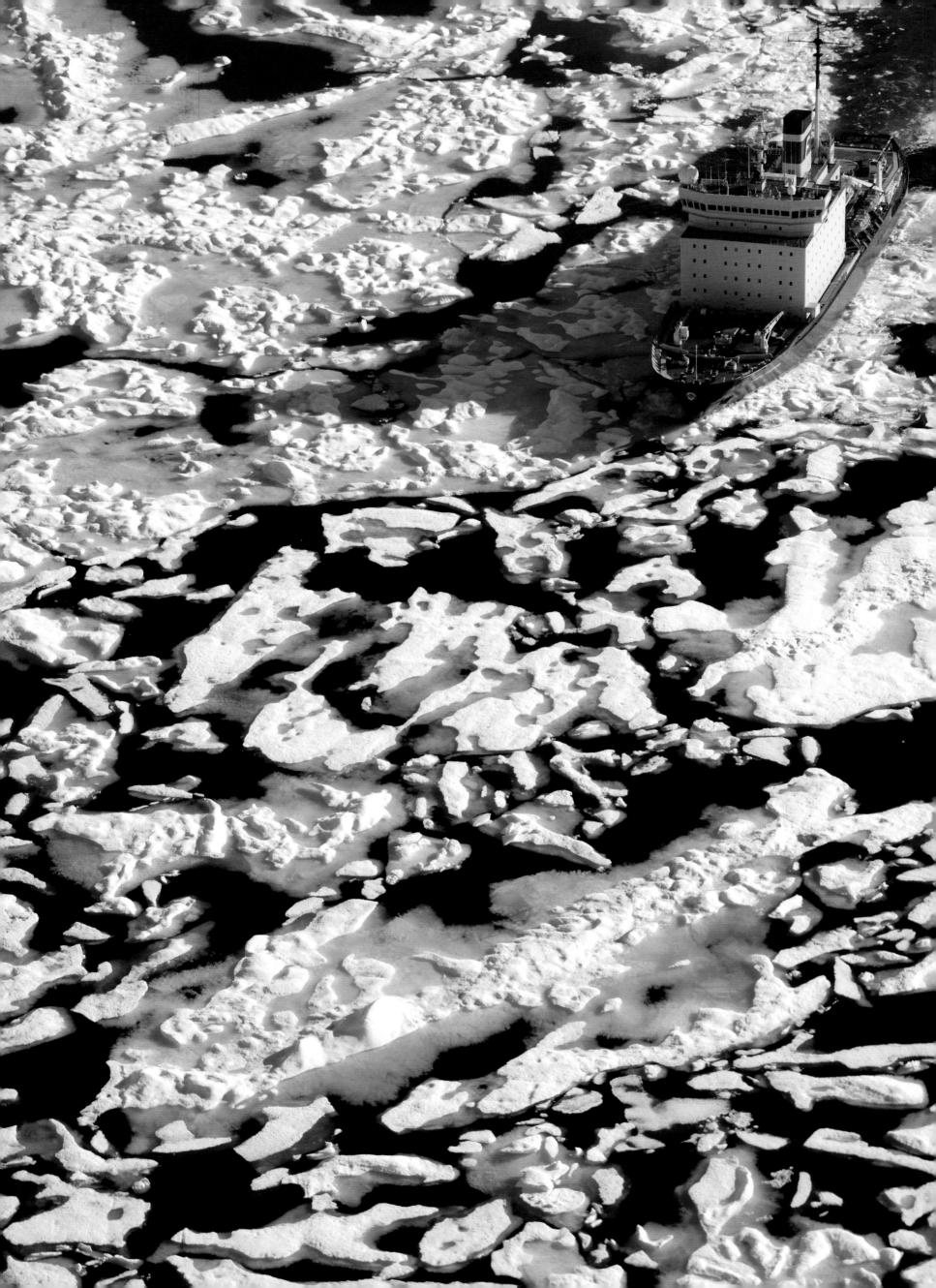

Gila monster. **Sonora, Mexico** ︿ |

Night ice climbing. **British Columbia, Canada** ^ |

Horsetail Falls. **Yosemite National Park, California, USA** >

Grand View Point. **Utah, USA** ∧

Atlantic walrus. **Repulse Bay, Canada** ^ |

Sunbathing walrus. **Foxe Basin, Canada** ▲ ⏐

Ancient wood. **Inyo National Forest, California, USA** ^ |

Braided river channels. **Alaska** >

Sequoia National Park. **California, USA** ^ |

Mallards in flight. **Massapequa, Long Island, New York** ^ |

Corcovado National Park. **Costa Rica** ^ |

Shiprock. **New Mexico, USA** › |

Yellow eyelash viper. **Manzanillo, Limon, Costa Rica**   ^ |

Chisos Mountains. **Texas, USA** ˄ |

Falls gold. **Shenandoah National Park, Virginia, USA** ˃

Roseate Spoonbill. **Florida, USA**   ▲ |

Grand Canyon. **Arizona, USA** ^ |

~ INDEX ~

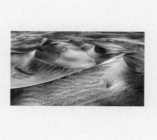

Thuringian Forest.
Thuringia, Germany

The 'green heart of Germany', Thuringia is a small, densely forested state, well known for wilderness, winter sports and Germany's most famous hiking trail, the 169.3km Rennsteig.

Page 59
PHOTOGRAPHER
Matt Munro

Lago di Carezza.
Italian Dolomites

This spring-fed puddle is famed for its stunning colours. The 'lake of the rainbow', fringed by dense fir-tree forest, reflects Latemar – the westernmost mountain of the Dolomites.

Page 60
PHOTOGRAPHER
Matt Munro

Serra de Tramuntana.
Mallorca, Spain

Seen here bathed in the light of the setting sun, the Serra de Tramuntana mountain range shelters much of Mallorca from the fierce tramuntana wind. It offers great hiking and biking.

Page 61
PHOTOGRAPHER
Marcos Molina | Getty Images

Camargue horses.
Southern France

An ancient equine breed, these semi-wild horses are indigenous to the marshes of the Rhône delta, a vital and protected wetland in the south of France.

Page 62
PHOTOGRAPHER
Danita Delimont | Getty Images

Icebergs.
Jökulsárlón, Iceland

Wind-whipped waves jostle icebergs on the wild waters of Jökulsárlón, an extensive glacial lake in southeast Iceland, found at the head of the Breiðamerkurjökull glacier.

Page 63
PHOTOGRAPHER
Olimpio Fantuz | 4Corners

Geirangerfjord and Seven Sisters waterfall.
Sunnmøre, Norway

This spectacular fjord is 15km long. Opposite the Seven Sisters is the tumbling, bumbling 'Suitor' waterfall, said to be trying to woo the sisters.

Page 64
PHOTOGRAPHER
Justin Foulkes

Landmannalaugar.
Fjallabak Nature Reserve, South Iceland

Rhyolite mountains create an other-worldly landscape on the edge of a 500-year-old lava field located at the northern end of a popular hiking trail.

Page 65
PHOTOGRAPHER
Luciano Gaudenzio | 4Corners

Simeto River.
Sicily, Italy

The sky busts into flames above the Simeto, as Mount Etna broods in the background, contemplating its next outburst. At 3329m, Etna is Europe's tallest active volcano.

Page 66
PHOTOGRAPHER
Fortunato Gatto | 4Corners

Central Balkan National Park.
Bulgaria

The rising sun paints the mountain a range of hues as wild horses enjoy breakfast. This park is home to myriad rare and endangered species.

Page 68
PHOTOGRAPHER
Maya Karkalicheva | Getty Images

Great white pelicans.
Danube Delta, Romania

A bird that can weigh up to 15kg, the white pelican looks graceful as it floats towards Europe's biggest river delta, on water that has passed through eight countries before Romania.

Page 69
PHOTOGRAPHER
David Fettes | Getty Images

Continental drift.
Silfra Crack, Iceland

Visibility extends over 100m in this exciting fissure, where you can dive directly in the crack between two continental plates, blowing bubbles from North America to Eurasia.

Page 70
PHOTOGRAPHER
Werner Van Steen | Getty Images

Soca River.
Primorska, Slovenia

Turquoise with limestone sediment from snowmelt, the Soca tumbles through the Julian Alps before gushing into Italy. The river retains its colour for its entire 138km length.

Page 71
PHOTOGRAPHER
Danita Delimon | Getty Images

Hubertus Viaduct.
Rhineland-Palatinate, Germany

On the steep section of the stunning Hunsrück railway's route between Boppard and Boppard-Buchholz, trains still cross this 150m-long viaduct.

Page 72
PHOTOGRAPHER
Westend61 | Getty Images

Karwendel Range.
Bavarian Alps, Germany

The Karwendel is the largest range of the Northern Limestone Alps, which extend from Austria into Bavaria. Looking from Herzogstand, this vista shows Lake Walchen.

Page 74
PHOTOGRAPHER
Cornelia Doerr | Getty Images

Fajã Grande, Flores Island.
Azores, Portugal

Waterfalls cascade over a volcanic wall near Fajã Grande, the westernmost settlement in Europe, 1360km from mainland Portugal across the Atlantic.

Page 75
PHOTOGRAPHER
Joel Santos | Getty Images

The Old Man of Storr.
Isle of Skye, Scotland

In heavenly harsh surroundings, the iconic Old Man of Storr rock formation looks out over Loch Leathan and the Sound of Raasay from its vantage point on the Trotternish peninsula.

Page 76
PHOTOGRAPHER
Sebastian Wasek | 4Corners

Nividic Lighthouse.
Ile d'Ouessant, France

Waves slam into one of a trio of lighthouses off Ushant, an island at the junction of France's northwestern extremities and the southwestern end of the English Channel.

Page 77
PHOTOGRAPHER
Jean-Marie Liot | Getty Images

Autumnal forest.
Velebit, Croatia

The Adriatic coast-side of Velebit, Croatia's largest mountain range, is barren, but the interior-facing Lika side has wood-covered slopes that ignite with autumnal hues.

Page 78
PHOTOGRAPHER
Romulic-Stojcic | Getty Images

Holuhraun eruption.
Icelandic Highlands

In August 2014, after 1600 quakes in 48 hours, a fissure opened between Bárðarbunga volcano and the Holuhraun lava field, which continued spewing magma until February 2015.

Page 79
PHOTOGRAPHER
Johnathan Ampersand Esper | Getty Images

Goðafoss waterfall.
Bárðardalur, Iceland

Even in a land so blessed with natural wonders, the 'waterfall of the gods' is a spectacular sight, as the Skjálfandafljót River rushes over a 30m-wide horseshoe-shaped 12m-drop.

Page 80
PHOTOGRAPHER
Fortunato Gatto | 4Corners

Red kite in flight.
Chiltern Hills, England

In the 1990s, red kites were reintroduced to England when several birds from Spain were released in the Chilterns – an Area of Outstanding Natural Beauty in the green southeast.

Page 82
PHOTOGRAPHER
Tim Flach | Getty Images

Icelandic horse.
Iceland

A small, tough breed, Icelandic horses are descended from animals brought in by ancient Norse settlers. Importing horses is illegal, so they are the only breed in the country.

Page 83
PHOTOGRAPHER
Tim Flach | Getty Images

Col de Bavella.
Corsica, France

The Col de Bavella is overlooked by the imposing silhouette of one of the most striking landscape features in the south of Corsica: the sharp points of Aiguilles de Bavella.

Page 84
PHOTOGRAPHER
David Noton | Alamy

Isle of Harris.
Outer Hebrides, Scotland

Channels snake their way through the Rodel saltmarsh. The Isle of Harris is actually the southern, mountainous part of the Lewis and Harris island.

Page 86
PHOTOGRAPHER
David Clapp | Getty Images

Atlantic coast, Cornwall.
England, UK

Powerful waves explode on a wild-weather hardened headland in Cornwall, where England's exposed westward poking toe feels the full force of the awesome Atlantic.

Page 87
PHOTOGRAPHER
David Clapp | Getty Images

The Milky Way.
Kiruna, Sweden

Our galactic neighbours show their twinkling faces as the Milky Way rises above a forest of Scandinavian pines near the Lapland settlement of Kiruna, Sweden's northernmost town.

Page 88
PHOTOGRAPHER
David Clapp | Getty Images

Life at Land's End.
Cornwall, England

Coastal flowers bloom on the westernmost edge of England, with a view towards Enys Dodnan arch, the Armed Knight rock formation and the Land's End Visitors Centre.

Page 90
PHOTOGRAPHER
David Clapp | Getty Images

Snowdonia.
North Wales

A gaggle of Eurasian wigeon, a species of dabbling duck, roost on the serpentine meander of a river, with the sun setting on the hills of Snowdonia in the background.

Page 91
PHOTOGRAPHER
David Clapp | Getty Images

Wayag Island.
Raja Ampat, Indonesia

Famed for the quality of its diving, with astonishing atolls and underwater wildlife, the island-peppered lagoon around Pulau Wayag in West Papua is easy on the eye from above too.

Page 93
PHOTOGRAPHER
Ethan Daniels | Getty Images

Crystal Cave.
Dead Sea, Jordan

In a beguiling bejewelled cave on the Jordanian shore, somewhere near Zara, splashing Dead Sea waves have left a decorative layer of salty crystals and stalactites.

Page 94
PHOTOGRAPHER
George Steinmetz | Corbis

Dead Sea shore.
Ein Gedi, Israel

The Dead Sea waterline is dropping about 1m per year. As it recedes, fresh groundwater dissolves subterranean salt deposits, resulting in sinkholes pockmarking the coast.

Page 95

PHOTOGRAPHER
George Steinmetz | Corbis

Subterranean explorers.
Phong Nha-Ke Bang National Park, Vietnam

Spelunkers enter Hang Son Doong, the planet's biggest cave, which has a single chamber more than 5km long, 200m high and 150m wide.

Page 96

PHOTOGRAPHER
Ryan Deboodt | Alamy

Break dancing.
Nias Island, North Sumatra

A surfer takes the Indian Ocean firmly by the hand and gets jiggy with a big wave on the coast of the idyllic Indonesian isle of Nias.

Page 98

PHOTOGRAPHER
Paul Kennedy | Getty Images

Longtailed macaque.
Bali, Indonesia

An infant longtailed macaque tucks into a piece of fruit in the arms of its mother, within the Ubud Monkey Forest nature reserve and Hindu temple in the village of Padangtegal.

Page 99

PHOTOGRAPHER
Matt Munro

Bromo Tengger Semeru National Park.
Jawa island, Indonesia

Centred on a massif containing smoking Mt Semeru (3676m), the highest on Java, this park is covered by the caldera of an ancient volcano, Tengger.

Page 100

PHOTOGRAPHER
Tuul & Bruno Morandi | 4Corners

Juvenile gaur.
Kanha National Park, Madhya Pradesh, India

The Indian bison, or. gaur, is the world's biggest bovine, but size isn't everything when you live in a national park famous for its Royal Bengal tigers.

Page 101

PHOTOGRAPHER
Nicholas Reuss | Getty Images

Huangshan Mountains.
Anhui, China

A bright new day is announced in the highlands of eastern China, as a sensational sunrise sets the pine trees ablaze, bathing Huangshan (Yellow Mountain) in a golden glow.

Page 102

PHOTOGRAPHER
Luigi Vaccarella | 4Corners

Forest of the fireflies.
Okayama, Japan

In an extraordinary display of bioluminescence rarely seen above water, fireflies set a glade aglitter in a temporarily enchanted forest, signalling the start of the Japanese summer.

Page 104

PHOTOGRAPHER
Trevor Williams | Getty Images

Camels up close.
Gansu Province, China

A vital strand of the Silk Road threaded through Gansu, which was once trafficked by camel caravans taking the textile to Europe. The animals are still used to convoy goods here.

Page 106

PHOTOGRAPHER
Danita Delimont | Getty Images

Ships of the desert.
Badain Jaran, Mongolia

A camel train crosses the megadunes of China's third largest desert, home to a 500m sand mountain. 'Singing dunes' – a mysterious acoustic phenomenon – are also here.

Page 107

PHOTOGRAPHER
Danita Delimont | Getty Images

Ao Phang-Nga National Marine Park.
Thailand

Established in 1981 and covering an area of 400 sq km, Ao Phang-Nga Marine National Park is noted for its classic karst scenery.

Page 108

PHOTOGRAPHER
Catherine Sutherland

Valley of the Geysers.
Kamchatka, Russia

With 500-plus hot springs, bubbling mud pits, volcanoes and geysers, Kamchatka is justifiably called the Land of Fire and Ice. It also has the planet's biggest brown bears.

Page 110

PHOTOGRAPHER
Frans Lanting | Getty Images

Rocks and rollers.
Lampung, Indonesia

At the southern extremity of Sumatra, Lampung – home to Mt Krakatau, which killed thousands when it erupted in 1883 – is a place where nature visibly flexes its muscles.

Page 111

PHOTOGRAPHER
Cinegolistic | Getty Images

Rose Valley.
Cappadocia, Turkey

An audience of astonishing rock formations – known as fairy chimneys – point towards a cast of stars in the night sky above Central Turkey's famous desert landscape.

Page 112

PHOTOGRAPHER
David Clapp | Getty Images

Potanina Glacier.
Altai Tavan Bogd National Park, Mongolia

Of the 20 or so glaciers that creep through the Altai range, the 14km-long Potanina glacier around Altai Tavan Bogd mountain is the largest.

Page 114

PHOTOGRAPHER
Tim Draper | 4Corners

Kaluts at sunrise
Iran

Kaluts – giant wind-sculpted sandcastles – stand sentinel in the Dasht-e Lut desert north of Kerman, blasted by a relentless sun that makes this one of the planet's driest spots.

Page 115

PHOTOGRAPHER
Tim Gerard Barker | Getty Images

Ice-climbing Sounkyo Gorge.
Hokkaido, Japan

Ice climbers cling onto a frozen waterfall in Daisetsuzan National Park in the mountainous heart of Japan's northern island.

Page 116

PHOTOGRAPHER
Andrew Peacock | Alamy

Bubble coral shrimp.
Bunaken National Marine Park, Indonesia

This translucent subspecies of shrimp is a specialist marine cleaner, exclusively sprucing bubble coral, found across Indo-Pacific reefs.

Page 118

PHOTOGRAPHER
Corrado Giavara | 4Corners

Cathedral of coral.
Bunaken National Marine Park, Indonesia

Sulawesi's marine refuge boasts almost 400 species of kaleidoscopic coral, as well as a wealth of fish, mollusc, reptile and mammal life.

Page 119

PHOTOGRAPHER
Settimio Cipriani | 4Corners

Korowai tribesman.
Southeastern Papua, Indonesia

Korowai men ascend thick ironwood trees by gripping vines with their hands and splayed toes. Here the man seeks black ants for fish bait.

Page 120

PHOTOGRAPHER
George Steinmetz | Corbis

Aoraki/Mt Cook.
South Island, New Zealand

The vista across Canterbury Plains towards NZ's Southern Alps is simultaneously a gift and an order to put on some boots and go explore.

Page 123

PHOTOGRAPHER
Matt Munro

Termite tower.
East Kimberley, Western Australia

Amid spiky spinifex grass, which carpets large parts of outback Australia in nests of nature's knitting needles, a termite mound stands proud.

Page 124

PHOTOGRAPHER
Don Fuchs | Getty Images

Heron among boulders.
Otago, South Island, New Zealand

On Koekohe Beach, the Moeraki Boulders have generated many Maori legends. Some claim they are eel baskets washed ashore from a mythical wrecked canoe.

Page 125

PHOTOGRAPHER
Massimo Ripani | 4Corners

Cruising crocodile.
Papua New Guinea

PNG is home to several species of crocodile, including the estuarine (saltwater) crocodile, thought to have been responsible for 65 fatal attacks on humans since 1958.

Page 126

PHOTOGRAPHER
Roberto Rinaldi | 4Corners

White Island.
Bay of Plenty, New Zealand

Whakaari, New Zealand's most active volcano, sits 48km from the North Island. The cone has huffed and puffed since Captain Cook first spotted it in 1769.

Page 128

PHOTOGRAPHER
Ed Norton | Getty Images

Whale encounter.
Kaikoura, South Island, New Zealand

Currents that swirl around the Kaikoura Peninsula attract a plethora of marine life. The sperm whale viewing here is arguably the best in the world.

Page 129

PHOTOGRAPHER
Chris Adam | Getty Images

Bouncing kangaroos.
Cape Le Grand, Western Australia

It's not unusual to see red roos bounding along the beach at Lucky Bay. When they're all bounced out, they forage through the seaweed for dinner.

Page 130

PHOTOGRAPHER
John W Banagan | Getty Images

Giant barrel sponge.
Papua New Guinea

A diver is dwarfed by a giant barrel sponge. These huge animals (yes, sponges are animals) are called 'redwood of the reef' because they can live for more than 2000 years.

Page 131

PHOTOGRAPHER
Roberto Rinaldi | 4Corners

Sopoaga Falls.
Western Samoa

Gushing from the heart of an almost surreally verdant and fecund forest, the powerful Sopoago Falls tumble into a gorgeous gorge near Lotofaga village in Samoa.

Page 132

PHOTOGRAPHER
Rothenborg Kyle | Getty Images

Windswept macrocarpas.
The Catlins, South Island, New Zealand

The Monterey cypress (known locally as macrocarpas) is a tough tree, but it bows to the force of the wind that blasts Waipawa Point's shoreline.

Page 133

PHOTOGRAPHER
Paul Kennedy | Getty Images

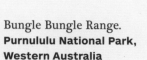

Portuguese-man-o-war.
Australia

Referred to as bluebottles by their victims – the 10,000 surfers and swimmers of Australia's East Coast who get stung every year – the man-o-war packs a painful punch.

Page 134

PHOTOGRAPHER
Karen Gowlett-Holmes | Getty Images

Hill Inlet, Whitsunday Islands National Park
Queensland, Australia

Its fine white sand lapped by the Coral Sea's turquoise waters, Hill Inlet is one of many idyllic spots scattered across the Whitsundays' 74 islands.

Page 135

PHOTOGRAPHER
Andrew Watson | Getty Images

Bungle Bungle Range.
Purnululu National Park, Western Australia

Revered by indigenous people for millennia, the 350-million-year-old red beehive-shaped peaks in east Kimberley are now World Heritage listed.

Page 136

PHOTOGRAPHER
Auscape/UIG | Getty Images

Lesser Bird of Paradise.
Papua New Guinea

In the Western Highlands of Papua New Guinea – a nirvana for birdwatchers – a Lesser Bird of Paradise puts on a feather-ruffling display to attract a mate to his lek.

Page 138

PHOTOGRAPHER
David Tipling | Getty Images

Curio Bay rollers.
South Island, New Zealand

At Curio Bay in the Catlins, the ocean rushes in from Antarctica with such fury it's no wonder that the local fossil forest is petrified.

Page 139

PHOTOGRAPHER
Rolf Hicker | Getty Images

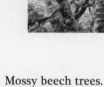

Great Barrier Reef.
Queensland, Australia

The planet's biggest living, breathing entity is a 2300km-long, incredibly complex ecosystem, comprised of more than 3000 individual reef systems, islands and coral cays.

Page 140

PHOTOGRAPHER
Peter Adams | Getty Images

Flying foxes.
Northern Territory, Australia

Fruit bats spread their wings in the night air above Mataranka, gateway town to Elsey National Park and a pitstop on the 2834km Stuart Highway.

Page 142

PHOTOGRAPHER
Regis Martin | Getty Images

Mossy beech trees.
Mt Aspiring National Park, New Zealand

A wild walker's wonderland, the rain-prone southwest flank of the South Island is also an ideal habitat for moss – of which New Zealand has 550 species.

Page 143

PHOTOGRAPHER
Philip Lee Harvey

Cassowary.
Australia

Indigenous to northern Queensland, the large, flightless cassowary is one of the most primitive birds in the world, being little evolved from a dinosaur.

Page 144

PHOTOGRAPHER
Tristan Brown | Getty Images

Russle lupines.
Lake Tekapo, South Island, New Zealand

Even blooming lupines face competition from the view that blossoms as the sun sets the snow-covered Southern Alps ablaze around Lake Tekapo.

Page 145

PHOTOGRAPHER
AtomicZen | Getty Images

Wielangta forest.
Tasmania, Australia

A mist descends on Wielangta, populated by eucalypts, eagles, bandicoots and the battle cries of generations of activists who protected this rainforest from the logging industry.

Page 146

PHOTOGRAPHER
Rob Blakers | Getty Images

Scuba school.
Mborokua, Solomon Islands

A jungle-cloaked volcanic isle, Mborokua is popular with divers seeking close encounters with marine life, such as this shoal of bigeye jacks.

Page 148

PHOTOGRAPHER
Rodger Klein | Getty Images

Beech tree.
Tasmania, Australia

Exclusive to the cool climes of Tasmania, this tangled deciduous beech tree puts on a spectacular display from April to May, segueing from rusty red through to splendid gold.

Page 149

PHOTOGRAPHER
Rob Blakers | Getty Images

Twisted tea tree.
Mornington Wildlife Sanctuary, Australia

This Western Australian sanctuary sits in the midst of the Central Kimberley bioregion, one of the world's last true wilderness areas.

Page 150

PHOTOGRAPHER
Auscape | Getty Images

The Corner of the World.
Nugget Point, South Island, New Zealand

The rocks extending from Nugget Point Lighthouse towards the cloud-streaked horizon line are like stepping stones to the edge of the Earth.

Page 151

PHOTOGRAPHER
Shan Shihan | Getty Images

Galahs.
Australia

A fiery flock of rose-breasted galahs flutter across the great brown land of Australia in a blush of colour and commotion. The charismatic birds are found across the continent.

Page 152
PHOTOGRAPHER
Martin Harvey | Getty Images

Kahurangi National Park.
South Island, New Zealand

The snow-sprinkled tops of the mountains in New Zealand's second largest park are reflected in the glasslike surface of the river.

Page 153
PHOTOGRAPHER
Matt Munro

Lightning strike.
Queensland, Australia

In the tropical forest of Daintree National Park, in the Far North of Queensland, a circle of scorched trees is evidence of a lightning strike, which can start bush fires.

Page 154
PHOTOGRAPHER
Peter Adams | Alamy

Melting moment.
Wilhelmina Bay, Antarctica

Under pressure from the never-setting summer sun, an iceberg slowly releases its water back to the embrace of the mighty Southern Ocean.

Page 157
PHOTOGRAPHER
Paul Souders | Getty Images

Errera Channel.
Antarctic Peninsula

A leopard seal cavorts in its extreme submarine playground on the frigid fringe of an other-worldly continent, utterly at home in an element where it occupies apex predator status.

Page 158
PHOTOGRAPHER
Michael S Nolan | Getty Images

Iceberg.
Antarctic Peninsula

Earth's coldest, driest, windiest place is a shapeshifting continent, growing and (increasingly) receding in size as seasons turn and tongues of water lick at its extremities.

Page 160
PHOTOGRAPHER
Andrew Peacock | Getty Images

Southern Ocean.
Antarctica

An icebreaker cuts through the pack ice around Antarctica, leaving a sea road in its wake. The jagged jigsaw won't take long to reform, though, erasing all trace of the intruder.

Page 161
PHOTOGRAPHER
Frans Lanting | Getty Images

False Cape Renard and Humphries Heights.
Graham Land, Antarctica

The serrated profile of False Cape Renard saws through the frozen mirror of the Southern Ocean off the northwest coast of the Kiev Peninsula.

Page 162
PHOTOGRAPHER
Andrew Peacock | Getty Images

Gentoo penguin.
Antarctica

A gentoo penguin shelters behind the bones of a whale skeleton. The most well-known gentoo – identified by a bonnet-like white stripe across its head – is the adélie penguin.

Page 164
PHOTOGRAPHER
Axel Fassio | Getty Images

An ice flow with seal.
Wilhelmina Bay, Antarctica

A seal rests on an ice floe but must beware of local pods of predatory orca that have learned how to sweep them off and into the ocean.

Page 165
PHOTOGRAPHER
Pete Seaward

King Penguins.
South Georgia

Adult and young King penguins, a quarter of a million of them, congregate on Salisbury Plain on South Georgia in the southern Atlantic ocean.

Page 166
PHOTOGRAPHER
Pete Seaward

Violet-tailed sylph.
Tandayapa Valley, Ecuador

A male hummingbird visits flowers of epiphytic Heath in an Andean cloud forest. The birds pollinate the flowers they collect nectar from.

Page 169
PHOTOGRAPHER
Michael & Patricia Fogden | Getty Images

Jaguar.
South America

The patch of America's largest feline extends from southwest USA through Central America into northern Argentina. Sightings are rare, but it looms large in indigenous mythology.

Page 170
PHOTOGRAPHER
Mike Hill | Getty Images

Perito Moreno Glacier.
Santa Cruz, Argentina

Chunks of ice calve from Perito Moreno Glacier in Los Glaciares National Park. The 30km-long tongue of ice is one of 48 glaciers extending from the Southern Patagonian Ice Field.

Page 171
PHOTOGRAPHER
Bruno Buongiorno Nardelli | Getty Images

Waterlilies at sunrise.
Pantanal, Brazil

The world's largest tropical wetland, Pantanal squelches, drips and flows over an area between 140,000 and 195,000 sq km, 80 percent of which is submerged in the wet season.

Page 172
PHOTOGRAPHER
Nat Photos | Getty Images

Parque Nacional dos Lençóis Maranhenses.
Maranhão, Brazil

Despite its desert-like looks, this dune-dotted landscape gets plenty of rain. It's prevented from draining by impermeable rock, forming colourful lagoons.

Page 173
PHOTOGRAPHER
Giordano Cipriani | 4Corners

Paraglider.
Iquique Province, Chile

A paraglider surfs the elements high above the Pacific, riding thermals generated by the Montanhas de Iquique, a range that rises suddenly behind a crescent of Chilean coastline.

Page 174
PHOTOGRAPHER
Lucas Nishimoto | Getty Images

Park Nacional Natural Tayrona.
Colombia

Lying on Colombia's Caribbean coast, this park is home to more than 50 endangered species but visitors are more likely to find gorgeous beaches.

Page 176
PHOTOGRAPHER
Jane Sweeney | Corbis

Desert camelids.
Atacama Desert, Chile

Llamas are mountain plateau animals but the Atacama hasn't enough water to support them. However, their smaller cousins, the guanaco and vicuña, are customised desert dwellers.

Page 177
PHOTOGRAPHER
Westend61 | Getty Images

Rio de Janeiro.
Brazil

A storm unleashes its fury over Brazil's most famous city, no stranger to extreme weather. In 2014, a lightening strike chipped the thumb of the iconic Christ the Redeemer.

Page 178
PHOTOGRAPHER
Aldo Pavan | 4Corners

Poison frog.
Río Marañón, Peru

Found across South America, these amphibians are often called poison dart frogs because Indigenous people have used their toxic secretions on the tips of blow darts.

Page 179
PHOTOGRAPHER
Brad Wilson | Getty Images

Iguazu Falls.
Brazil

Although boat trips can take you up close to the dramatic impact zone of Iguazu, only a helicopter ride will truly bring home the magnificence of the falls' 2.7km-long, curled lip.

Page 180
PHOTOGRAPHER
Guido Cozzi | 4Corners

Shoal of piraputanga.
Mato Grosso do Sul, Brazil

The 'Thick Forest of the South' is rich in wildlife above and below the surface of the giant Pantanal wetland dominating the state. Fish thrive here.

Page 182
PHOTOGRAPHER
Franco Banfi | Getty Images

Eruption of Calbuco.
Los Lagos, Chile

Seen here from Puerto Montt, Calbuco volcano blew its top in April 2015, sending a smoke column 20km into the air and prompting the evacuation of 1500 nearby inhabitants.

Page 183
PHOTOGRAPHER
Alex Vidal Brecas | Corbis

Toucan.
Cartagena, Colombia

Found in the northern and Caribbean parts of South America, the toucan's colourful bill is used as a fencing weapon when sorting out the pecking order of a social group.

Page 184
PHOTOGRAPHER
Gabriele Croppi | 4Corners

Yavarí River.
The Amazon, Peru

For 800km, this tributary of the Amazon river forms the border between Brazil and Peru. It's an outstanding, if adventurous, location for wildlife watching and is navigable by canoe.

Page 185
PHOTOGRAPHER
Mark Bowler | Getty Images

Moai.
Easter Island, Chile

Seven stone statues, or moai, look out to sea from Aku Akivi, in Rapa Nui National Park. The island society's fate is a cautionary tale about how not to deplete natural resources.

Page 186
PHOTOGRAPHER
Eric Lafforgue

Paílón del Diablo.
Baños de Agua Santa, Ecuador

Negotiating the winding walkway to the 'Cauldron of the Devil' waterfall on the Pastaza River is almost as exciting as beholding the cascade itself.

Page 187
PHOTOGRAPHER
Westend61 | Getty Images

Paine Massif.
Torres Del Paine, Chile

The main attraction of Chilean Patagonia, this National Park has lakes, mountains, glaciers and rivers. Paine Massif, a trio of granite peaks, is crowned by 2884m Paine Grande.

Page 188
PHOTOGRAPHER
Matt Munro

Whitewater kayaker.
Rio Azul, Chile

Chile caters for every possible adventure sport. Here, a kayaker paddles the Rio Azul near Futaleufu. A class IV river, the Azul's most dangerous rapid is the 'Cheese Grater'.

Page 190
PHOTOGRAPHER
Karl Weatherly | Getty Images

Andean condor.
Colca Canyon, Peru

Twice as deep as the Grand Canyon, the Colca is one of the world's biggest. Carrion-eating condors catch rising thermals and glide effortlessly high above the Colca River.

Page 191
PHOTOGRAPHER
Bjorn Holland | Getty Images

Sunrise, Salar de Uyuni.
Bolivia

The world's largest salt flat is always dramatic, but at dawn it's mind blowing: 10,582 sq km of salt and nothing else bar the odd cacti-covered island and several species of flamingo.

Page 192
PHOTOGRAPHER
Westend61 | Getty Images

Pink river dolphin.
Manaus, Brazil

One of the Amazon's many wonders, these animals have a brain capacity 40 percent larger than humans, but face threats from habitat loss, pollution and river traffic.

Page 193
PHOTOGRAPHER
Morales | Getty Images

La Cascada de Peguche.
Otavalo, Ecuador

At the sacred waterfall of Peguche – an 18m cascade – purification baths take place in the days leading to the Andean summer solstice celebration Inti Raymi, dating to Inca times.

Page 194
PHOTOGRAPHER
Guy Edwardes | Getty Images

Cordillera de Chicas.
Bolivia

Amid the Cordillera de Chicas' Wild West topography, Butch Cassidy and the Sundance Kid pulled off their last robbery about 40km from Tupiza, at Huaca Huañusca (Dead Cow).

Page 195
PHOTOGRAPHER
Simon Montgomery | Getty Images

Galápagos sea lion.
Galápagos Islands, Ecuador

The chirpy nature of the Galápagos sea lion (smaller than their Californian cousins) has led people to dub them the Islands' 'welcoming party'.

Page 196
PHOTOGRAPHER
Franco Banfi | Getty Images

Hummingbird drawing.
Nazca, Peru

The Nazca Lines are supersized geoglyphs of bird and animal life etched in the desert floor. Experts believe they were created by the Nazca culture, 400-650 AD.

Page 197
PHOTOGRAPHER
Fridmar Damm | 4Corners

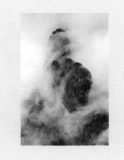

Tepui.
Venezuela

Clouds flow over the top of a tepui. Tepuis, such as Mt Roraima – the inspiration for Sir Arthur Conan Doyle's The Lost World – are tall, steep-sided plateaus in Venezuela's south.

Page 198
PHOTOGRAPHER
Martin Harvey | Alamy

Iguazu Falls.
Argentina

These waterfalls straddle the border between Argentina and Brazil. There are up to 300 separate falls as the Iguazu river rushes over the Paraná Plateau.

Page 199
PHOTOGRAPHER
Matt Munro

Banff National Park.
Alberta, Canada

Driftwood gathers around Moraine Lake. The mountains that crown this view were originally named numerically 1-10 in the Nakoda language, but most have been rebranded.

Page 201
PHOTOGRAPHER
Pietro Canali | 4Corners

Cactus.
Mexico

Native to Mexico, this small cactus is covered in short golden spines. Mexico is home to the world's tallest cactus variety, the cardon, which can grow to a height of 20m.

Page 202
PHOTOGRAPHER
Yvette Cardozo | Getty Images

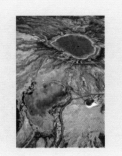

Excelsior geyser.
Yellowstone National Park, Wyoming, USA

From above, it looks like the surface of Mars, but this isn't sci-fi. The Excelsior geyser pool emits up to 17,000 litres of near-boiling water every minute.

Page 203
PHOTOGRAPHER
Tom Murphy | Getty Images

Sol Duc Falls.
Washington, USA

The massive Olympic National Park offers some Olympic-scale challenges, but one easy walk leads to a mossy ravine shrouded in mist, where the Sol Duc River rumbles away all day.

Page 204
PHOTOGRAPHER
Michael Breitung | 4Corners

Bison and Grand Tetons.
Wyoming, USA

American bison (commonly called buffalo) migrate from Yellowstone National Park in winter. They are seen here in autum, grazing on the prairie below the Grand Teton Range.

Page 206
PHOTOGRAPHER
Matt Anderson | Getty Images

Whaler's Grave.
Marble Island, Hudson Bay, Canada

A bowhead whale's vertebrae marks a grave on this sacred Inuit isle, where, according to lore, visitors must crawl ashore... or die one year later.

Page 208
PHOTOGRAPHER
Paul Souders | Getty Images

Grey Whale.
British Columbia, Canada

Branded 'devil fish' by whalers, because of its fighting spirit, this large (15m) baleen whale was widely hunted, but is now showing signs of recovery.

Page 209
PHOTOGRAPHER
Jim Borrowman | Getty Images

Arches National Park.
Utah, USA

Beneath the stars, one of 2000 red sandstone rock arches is illuminated. The most famous is the fragile looking Delicate Arch. Rain erosion has caused 43 to collapse since 1977.

Page 210
PHOTOGRAPHER
Pete Saloutos | Getty Images

Na Pali Coast.
Kaua'i, Hawaii

Kaua'i has starred in 70-plus films, from *South Pacific* to *Jurassic Park*. Behind Na Pali Coast, the 'Garden Isle' boasts 10-mile-long Waimea Canyon, and Sleeping Giant ridge.

Page 211
PHOTOGRAPHER
Ignacio Palacios | Getty Images

Glacier patterns.
Wrangell-St Elias National Park, Alaska

The ice caps wrapped in the embrace of this park include a trio of glaciers: Nabesna, Hubbard and Malaspina, which is bigger than Rhode Island.

Page 212
PHOTOGRAPHER
Frans Lanting | Getty Images

Trafalgar Falls.
Dominica

Two waterfalls lie behind this leafy curtain: 'father', with a big 65m drop, and the 35m 'mother'. Hot thermal pools are accessible from the larger; the smaller has a plunge pool.

Page 213
PHOTOGRAPHER
Giovanni Simeone | 4Corners

Peggy's Cove.
Nova Scotia, Canada

A setting sun over St Margaret's Bay means the red lamp in Peggy's Cove Lighthouse will soon begin its life-saving turn. The winking lighthouse is an icon of Canada's Atlantic coast.

Page 214
PHOTOGRAPHER
Justin Foulkes

Cape Race.
Newfoundland, Canada

The Avalon Peninsula bares its fangs here, where rocks, fog and transatlantic shipping lanes have caused carnage. The Cape Race Lighthouse received the Titanic's distress call.

Page 215
PHOTOGRAPHER
Justin Foulkes

Bryce Canyon.
Utah, USA

Bryce Canyon's hoodoos stand bright and alert, like meerkats. The feature is actually a set of big natural amphitheatres, and the hoodoos are sculpted by weathering and water erosion.

Page 216
PHOTOGRAPHER
Marco Isler | Getty Images

Polar bear.
Hudson Bay, Canada

A bear stands in the morning sun surveying the shoreline for breakfast. Of the world's 19 polar bear populations, 13 are found in Canada, and Churchill in Hudson Bay is PB capital.

Page 218
PHOTOGRAPHER
Paul Souders | Getty Images

The Narrows.
Zion National Park, Utah, USA

A lone tree adds a green splash to the sandy hued Narrows, a tight section of a canyon tracing the North Fork of the Virgin River.

Page 219
PHOTOGRAPHER
Thomas Janisch | Getty Images

Go with the floe.
Northwest Territories, Canada

A modern icebreaker nudges across the Arctic gulf where the long-lost wreck of HMS Erebus was discovered in 2014. The ship disappeared in 1839.

Page 220
PHOTOGRAPHER
Daisy Gilardini | Getty Images

Gila monster.
Sonora, Mexico

One of the world's two species of poisonous lizard, gila monsters, found in the southwestern US and Sonora, are slow moving and pose little threat to humans.

Page 221
PHOTOGRAPHER
Tim Flach | Getty Images

Night ice climbing, Kootenay National Park.
British Columbia, Canada

Climbers cling to ice in Haffner Creek. It's a mecca for mixed climbing, but in winter ice axes and crampons are de rigueur.

Page 222
PHOTOGRAPHER
Paul Zizka | Getty Images

Firefalls.
Yosemite National Park, California, USA

For a February fortnight, the sunset transforms Yosemite's Horsetail Falls into a cascade of molten gold, as rays reflect off the granite behind the water.

Page 223
PHOTOGRAPHER
Putt Sakdhnagool | Getty Images

Grand View Point.
Utah, USA

Even trees twist around to see the sunset that gazes across a wide-angle Canyonlands National Park vista. The top photo-op is at the trailhead of an eponymous hiking route.

Page 224
PHOTOGRAPHER
Maurizio Rellini | 4Corners

Atlantic walrus.
Repulse Bay, Canada

A walrus rests on sea ice near Vansittart Island. The animals' tusks are used for fighting, to make and maintain holes in the ice, and to help them climb out of the water.

Page 226

PHOTOGRAPHER
Paul Souders | Getty Images

Sunbathing walrus.
Foxe Basin, Canada

Although first chartered in 1631, little is known about Foxe Basin in Nunavut, except that it is very popular with polar bears and walrus, with a 6000-strong herd of the latter.

Page 227

PHOTOGRAPHER
Louise Murray | Getty Images

Ancient wood.
Inyo National Forest, California, USA

The Ancient Bristlecone Pine Forest is where the world's oldest trees grow. The oldest tree is 5064 – it would have germinated in 3049 BC.

Page 228

PHOTOGRAPHER
Danita Delimont |
Getty Images

Braided river channels.
Wrangell-St Elias National Park, Alaska

America's largest national park encompasses four major mountain ranges, multiple icefields and glaciers, rivers, and myriad wild animals.

Page 229

PHOTOGRAPHER
Frans Lanting | Getty Images

Sequoia National Park.
California, USA

In western Sierra Nevada, the Giant Forest strides over 760 hectares of land, covered in giant sequoia groves. The tree can reach 80m in height and boast a 30m girth at its base.

Page 230

PHOTOGRAPHER
Giovanni Simeone | 4Corners

Mallards in flight.
Massapequa, Long Island, New York

A flock of mallard ducks splash along a creek in Massapequa. The mallard is the most abundant and wide-ranging duck on Earth.

Page 231

PHOTOGRAPHER
Vicki Jauron | Getty Images

Corcovado National Park.
Costa Rica

This Osa Peninsula park is one of the planet's most biologically diverse places. Rare inhabitants include jaguars, pumas, harpy eagles, silky anteaters and spider monkeys.

Page 232

PHOTOGRAPHER
Frans Lanting | Getty Images

Shiprock.
New Mexico, USA

The Anasazi (ancient Pueblo people) centred their civilisation around Shiprock. The monadnock (free-standing rock) shoots 482.5m from the desert floor.

Page 233

PHOTOGRAPHER
Justin Foulkes

Yellow eyelash viper.
Manzanillo, Limon, Costa Rica

Seen here among flower buds, this pit viper is found in various colours across Central America. Its name stems from the scales above its eyes.

Page 234

PHOTOGRAPHER
George Grall | Getty Images

Cougar.
Belize

Also known as mountain lions and pumas, cougars are found across the continent, from the Canadian Yukon through to Central America. This male was photographed in Belize.

Page 235

PHOTOGRAPHER
Frans Lanting | Getty Images

Chisos Mountains.
Texas, USA

A spiky clump of agave, a succulent plant suited to deserts, collects the evening dew as the sun sets across the face of the Chisos Mountains in Big Bend National Park.

Page 236

PHOTOGRAPHER
Willard Clay | Getty Images

Falls gold.
Shenandoah National Park, Virginia, USA

Autumn gets busy with its palette of browns and yellows in White Oak Canyon, deep in the embrace of Virginia's Shenandoah National Park.

Page 237

PHOTOGRAPHER
Deb Snelson | Getty Images

The Everglades.
Florida, USA

A boat negotiates the 'Glades', Florida's wetlands, a vast expanse of sawgrass marsh that covers the southern part of the state from Lake Okeechobee to Florida Bay.

Page 238

PHOTOGRAPHER
David Job | Getty Images

Roseate Spoonbill.
Florida, USA

Almost 1m tall, the pink-plumaged Spoonbill is one of North America's most striking birds. It inhabits southern wet-lands, swinging its bill through water in the hunt for prey.

Page 239

PHOTOGRAPHER
Steve Blandin | Getty Images

Grand Canyon.
Arizona, USA

A condor's eye view of the Grand Canyon, a fissure in the Colorado Plateau that splits the Arizona desert for 446km, reaching a depth of 1857m at points along the Colorado River.

Page 240

PHOTOGRAPHER
Busà Photography |
Getty Images

JACKET:

Tre Cime di Lavaredo
at sunset.
**Dolomiti di Sesto
Natural Park, Italy**

PHOTOGRAPHER
Anne Maenurm/NATURALIGHT/
SIME | 4Corners

Gemsbok.
**Naukluft National Park,
Namibia**

PHOTOGRAPHER
Martin Harvey | Getty Images

Sardine Run.
South Africa

PHOTOGRAPHER
Alexander Sofonov |
Getty Images

Namib Desert.
Namibia

PHOTOGRAPHER
Mariusz Kluzniak | Getty Images

Great Barrier Reef.
Australia

PHOTOGRAPHER
Peter Adams | Getty Images

CASE:

Nyiragongo Volcano.
**Democratic Republic of
the Congo**

PHOTOGRAPHER
Ryan Goebel | Getty Images

Elephant in Liwonde
National Park.
Southern Malawi

PHOTOGRAPHER
Jonathan Gregson

Wadi Rum.
Jordan

PHOTOGRAPHER
Tom Mackie

INTRODUCTION:

Quiver tree.
**Goegap NatureReserve,
South Africa**

PHOTOGRAPHER
Mark Read

Chugach Mountains.
Alaska, USA

PHOTOGRAPHER
Michael Heffernan

LONELY PLANET'S

WILD
WORLD

PUBLISHED

October 2015

MANAGING DIRECTOR

Piers Pickard

ASSOCIATE PUBLISHER

Robin Barton

ART DIRECTION

Daniel Di Paolo

LAYOUT

Johanna Lundberg

CAPTIONS

Patrick Kinsella

COPYEDITOR

Nick Mee

PRE-PRESS PRODUCTION

Ryan Evans

PRINT PRODUCTION

Larissa Frost

**PUBLISHED BY LONELY PLANET
PUBLICATIONS PTY LTD**

90 Maribyrnong St, Footscray,

Victoria 3011, Australia

ABN 36 005 607 983

ISBN 978 1 74360 748 0

PRINTED IN CHINA

10 9 8 7 6 5 4 3 2 1

AUSTRALIA

90 Maribyrnong St, Footscray, Victoria, 3011

PHONE 03 8379 8000 **FAX** 03 8379 8111

USA

150 Linden St, Oakland, CA 94607

PHONE 510 250 6400 **TOLL FREE** 800 275 8555

UNITED KINGDOM

240 Blackfriars Road, London, SE1 8NW

PHONE 020 3771 5100 **FAX** 020 3771 5101

MIX
Paper from responsible sources
FSC™ C021741

Paper in this book is certified against the Forest Stewardship Council™ standards. FSC™ promotes environmentally responsible, socially beneficial and economically viable management of the world's forests.

ISBN 978-1-74360-748-0

COVER JACKET:

Tre Cime di Lavaredo at sunset. **Dolomiti di Sesto Natural Park, Italy**

PHOTOGRAPHER
Anne Maenurm/ NATURALIGHT/SIME | 4Corners

Gemsbok. **Naukluft National Park, Namibia**

PHOTOGRAPHER
Martin Harvey | Getty Images

Sardine Run. **South Africa**

PHOTOGRAPHER
Alexander Sofonov | Getty Images

Namib Desert. **Namibia**

PHOTOGRAPHER
Mariusz Kluzniak | Getty Images

Great Barrier Reef. **Australia**

PHOTOGRAPHER
Peter Adams | Getty Images

Cheetah in a fig tree. **Maasai Mara, Kenya**

PHOTOGRAPHER
Frans Lanting | Corbis

CASE:

Nyiragongo Volcano. **Democratic Republic of the Congo**

PHOTOGRAPHER
Ryan Goebel | Getty Images

Elephant in Liwonde National Park. **Southern Malawi**

PHOTOGRAPHER
Jonathan Gregson

Wadi Rum. **Jordan**

PHOTOGRAPHER
Tom Mackie

INTRODUCTION:

Puffin in a snowstorm. **Norway**

PHOTOGRAPHER
Jan Vermeer | Getty Images

Chugach Mountains. **Alaska, USA**

PHOTOGRAPHER
Michael Heffernan